A HOLY POEMS

**Dedicated To
The True & Living God,
Yahweh**

My Savior, Lord Yeshua

**And His Precious
Holy Spirit
Ruach HaKodesh**

**My Apostle & Overseer
Dr. Dorothy J. Page**

PUBLISHED 2018
Dr. Kathleen B. Oden
Teaching By The Spirit Ministries

TABLE OF CONTENTS

BRAGGIN ABOUT MY GOD
EVERY STEP OF THE WAY
GOD'S HOLY BREATH
GOD'S LOVE
PRAISE HIS HOLY WORD
I FEEL IT BY THE SPIRIT
HE'S JUST, THAT KIND OF GOD
THANK YOU LORD
WARRIOR BRIDE
WHAT IS CHRISTMAS?
WHO IS MY SOULMATE?
A SPIRITUAL MOTHER
EL ELYON
I BLESS YOU, MY ELOHIM
STRENGTHEN ME O ELOHIM

BIOGRAPHY

BRAGGIN ABOUT MY GOD

My GOD is Wonderful,
He's Marvelous,
And He's the True and Living GOD too.

The earth is sooo big,
But not as big as, My GOD.
He's Wonderful, He's Marvelous,
And He's the True and Living GOD too.

I love shiny Diamonds,
But they don't shine, like My GOD.
He's Wonderful, He's Marvelous,
And He's the True and Living GOD too.

Through technology,
computers have advanced very far today.
But, they don't have the knowledge
of My GOD.
He's Wonderful, He's Marvelous,
And He's the True and Living GOD too.

The Hubble Telescope
can see deep into the universe.
But it still, can't see, like My GOD.
He's Wonderful, He's Marvelous,
And He's the True and Living GOD too.

This house I live in is Great!
Because it's the Temple of My GOD!
Is that not Wonderful?!
Is that not Marvelous?!
And, He's the True and Living GOD too.

My GOD is a good GOD!
Unfortunately, everyone does not know that.
Why? Because they don't know, My GOD.
They don't know that HE'S WONDERFUL!
They don't know that HE' MARVELOUS!
And the True and Living GOD too.

How about you?
Would you like to know JESUS?
I invite you to partake
of HIS goodness TODAY!
OOOH He's Wonderful,
And He's Marvelous,
And He's the True and Living GOD too!

That is why I have to say, I am sooo blessed,
To share My GOD with you TODAY.
And not just because He's Wonderful.
Not just because He's Marvelous,
And He's the True and Living GOD too!
But because HE'S COMING BACK SOON!
And because HE Loves You,
And wants to be your GOD too.

Yes, I'm braggin about My GOD!
I can't help it!
But before I go on my way,
I have to tell everybody about my God
before it's too late.
I've got to tell everybody
That He's still wonderful.
I've got to tell everybody
That He's still marvelous.
And I've got to tell everybody
that He's still the one and only
True and living God, still today!

2010

> Oh that men
> would praise the LORD for
> his goodness, and for his
> wonderful works
> to the children of men!
> Psalm 107:8

EVERY STEP OF THE WAY

We need the Lord,
Each and every day,
Every step, of the way!

We need the Lord,
All thru the night,
Each and every day,
Every step, of the way!

And, we need the Lord,
To give us courage to strive!
Each and every day,
Every step, of the way!

We even need the Lord,
To help us pray,
Each and every day,
Every step, of the way!

Yes, we need the Lord,
To give us comfort and joy!
Each and every day,
Every step, of the way!

*And we really need the Lord,
To help us walk right
and talk right,
Each and every day,
Every step, of the way!*

*We need the Lord,
When we get mad or feeling sad,
Each and every day,
Every step, of the way!*

*Can I say, we need the Lord,
To help us stay saved?
Each and every day,
Every step, of the way?*

*And we certainly need the Lord,
To protect us from harm,
Each and every day,
Every step, of the way!*

*We truly need the Lord,
To sound an alarm!
Each and every day,
Every step, of the way!*

And we definitely need the Lord,
To give us strength to obey,
Each and every day,
Every step, of the way!

We need the Lord,
To help us share His Holy Word!
Each and every day,
Every step, of the way!

We need the Lord,
For so many things!
And these are just a few,
That I need the Lord To Do!

How about you?
Do you need the Lord,
Each and every day,
Every step, of the way?

Just call on His name,
And you'll hear Him say!
I'M HERE WITH YOU!
Each and every day,
Every step, of the way!

6/14/2016

GOD'S HOLY BREATH

God's Breath is Holy,
Because Holy is He.
God's Holy Breath,
Is in every human being.

God gave man His Holy Breath,
And little animals too.
We breathe God's Holy Breath,
Everyday, fresh and new.

God's Holy Breath
Blesses man to even sing.
After all, it belongs to the King of Kings.

We pray for the sick,
Both morning and night.
Using God's Holy Breath,
Not our, own might.

We must be very careful,
When we use God's Holy Breath.
We don't want to shame Him,
Or cause Him regret.

But man seems to forget,
Whose breath, he is using.
When he speaks many words,
Without even thinking.

Man should be thankful everyday
We live and breathe.
Because we have God's Holy Breath,
Flowing, within our being.

God's Holy Breath,
Gives man power to create with speech.
So we must be mindful,
To create peace.

What would the world be like,
If everyone used,
The Power of God's Holy Breath,
To Spread the Good News?

12/31/16

GOD'S LOVE

God's love, gives us hope
We can hope thou, til the end.
His plan for us is built on love,
A plan, with an expected end.

Don't bother to look
for unconditional love,
From mother or father,
Sister or brother,
Or any, significant other.

Unconditional love
Cannot be won,
But you can get it for free,
From the only Begotten Son.

God's love has no strings!
To pull us or bind us up,
Is just not His thing.

God's love makes us bold,
If we love Him,
With all our hearts,
Mind and soul.

But first,
We must receive His love,
and be made whole.

When people feel empty
They need Christ, you see.
They need to ask the Holy Spirit,
Come, Fill me.

Some people try to buy love,
Just to say, "This is my love!"
But true love comes from above,
A love that no one, is worthy of.

What is love? God is love.
True love is He.
His love brings joy
And peace, and liberty.
There is no other love,
Where by man can be made free.

And God's love is free for everyone,
Including, you and me.

8/12/13

PRAISE HIS HOLY WORD

His Word is perfect,
So praise Him!
It never fails to perform,
Praise His Holy Word,
It goes, it touches,
It does not return void!

His Word heals, so praise Him!
He knows just what we need,
Praise His Holy Word!
It goes, it touches,
It does not return void!

His Word is pure, so praise Him!
It purifies both mind and soul,
Praise His Holy Word,
Because it goes, it touches,
It does not return void!

His Word comforts, so praise Him!
It soothes whatever pain
We may bare,
Praise His Holy Word!
It goes, it touches,
It does not return void!

Oooh His Word is precious today,
So praise Him!
It's worth more than I can say,
Oh praise His Holy Word
It goes, it touches,
It does not return void!

His Word teaches, so praise Him!
It faithfully shows us His way,
Praise His Holy Word,
Because it goes, it touches,
It does not return void!

His Word is powerful,
So praise Him!
It can do more
Than we ask or think.
Praise His Holy Word!
It goes, it touches,
It does not return void!

His Word saves, so praise Him!
And, it continues to save, even today,
Oh praise His Holy Word
It goes, it touches,
It does not return void!

His Word is final, so praise Him!
It cannot be stopped by man.
Praise His Holy Word,
Because it goes, it touches,
It does not return void!

And His Word is everlasting,
So praise Him!
Because it continues to work
in our life, everyday!
Praise his everlasting Holy word
It continues to go out,
It continues to touch,
And it never returns void!
So Praise, His Everlasting, Holy Word!

2012

> I have not concealed the words of the Holy One.
> Job 6:10

I FEEL IT BY THE SPIRIT

I feel it by the Spirit.
A change is coming.

I look up in the sky, I don't see it.
I feel it, by the Spirit,
A change is coming.

The leaves are falling,
the ant is crawling,
But i feel it, by the Spirit,
A change is coming.

A good change a bad change,
Who can know it.
I feel it, by the Spirit,
A change is coming.

A good change for the saints,
Not the ones who faint.
I feel it, by the Spirit,
A change is coming.

Don't be weary, and don't tarry!
Jesus is soon to come, hurry!
I feel it, by the Spirit,
A change is coming.

I feel the heat, hotter and hotter,
But He has my hand,
Throughout every matter.
I feel it, by the Spirit,
A change is coming.

Am I ready, am I done?
Only the potter knows, this one.
But I just feel it, by the Spirit,
A change is coming.

I am turned, this way and that,
Trying not to cry, He, would not want that,
I feel it, by the Spirit,
A change is coming.

And when it arrives,
I want to be waiting, like a Bride.
I want to feel it, by the Spirit.
A change is coming.

It feels exciting!
And it feels new.
He comes with a reward
For me and you!
I feel it, by the Spirit,
A change is coming.
To bring us out, to reign us in,
To bless and free,

And show us HIM!
I can feel it, by the Spirit,
A change is coming!

Are you ready?
Are you prepared?
Can you feel it, by the Spirit,
That a change is coming?

Let's receive it, let's welcome it!
God will make it ok.
But we have to feel it,
By the Spirit.
Because a change is coming, to stay.

8-18-2011

For as many as are led by the Spirit of God, they are the sons of God.
Romans 8:14

HE'S JUST, THAT KIND OF GOD

*He knew me and He drew me,
With a love that, really soothed me.
Why? He's just, that kind of God!*

*He never sleeps, no not ever.
Because He watches over me, forever.
Why? Because He's just, that kind of God!*

*He saw me from afar,
And pulled me closer to His big soft heart.
Yes, He's just, that kind of God!*

*He holds back the mighty sea,
While He tends to my, every need.
Can you believe?
He's just, that kind of God?*

*He is a preacher!
An all knowing teacher,
Who is so kind, to every creature!
Yes, He's just, that kind of God!*

*He came to win, the souls of men,
And was willing to die, for their sins!
Does man really know,
He's just, that kind of God?*

He was a lamb, a living sacrifice!
Among people, that were, none too nice!
Why? He's just, that kind of God!

He could have spoke,
But, He bowed His head.
And took those stripes, in my stead!
Oh Yes, He's just, that kind of God!

And then He was mocked!
As He carried that cross!
So that one day,
I would no longer be lost!
Why? He's just, that kind of God!

He died for me, but rose in three!
And now Jesus lives in me,
To display His mercy & love,
unconditionally!

All because,
He's just, that kind of God!

3/2016

THANK YOU LORD

"Thank You Lord"
"Thank You Lord"
"Thank You Lord"

I just can't stop saying, "Thank You Lord."
As I rise up, I say, "Thank You Lord."
But, if the mailman brings bad news,
It's so hard to say, "Thank You Lord."

During my busy day, I often stop,
To say, "Thank You Lord."
But when someone is rude on the phone,
it hurts to say, "Thank You Lord"
And if someone takes my parking spot,
I don't feel like saying, "Thank You Lord"

Sometimes I forget my shopping list,
But, I just say ok, "Thank You Lord."

As I enjoy my lunch, it's so easy to say,
"Thank You Lord."

But wow, how time flies,
my day almost gone,
but "Thank You Lord."

*And as evening draws nigh, I begin to sigh,
a great-full whew!"Thank You Lord."*

*Time to go to bed, my day is all done.
He blessed me so much,
I must say at least one,
"Thank You Lord."*

*But as I begin to kneel and remember all
that He has done, I say,*

*"Thank You Lord"
"Thank You Lord"
"Thank You Lord"
Not just one!*

8-18-2011

> Give thanks unto the LORD, call upon his name, make known his deeds among the people.
> 1 Chronicles 16:8

WARRIOR BRIDE

Warrior Bride, Warrior Bride!
Rise and shine
Warrior Bride, Warrior Bride!
It's your time!

Warrior Bride, Warrior Bride!
It's time to fight!
Not with your strength,
But God's, power and might!

Warrior Bride, Warrior Bride!
It's time to lead!
Go forth Warrior Bride,
With God speed!

Warrior Bride, Warrior Bride!
It's time to search the land!
Search for those,
Willing to stand!

Warrior Bride, Warrior Bride!
It's time to walk the walk!
No more time,
To just talk the talk!

Warrior Bride, Warrior Bride!
It's time to seize the day!
Don't just lay there!
Get up and pray!

Warrior Bride, Warrior Bride!
It's time to grab your sword!
Read the word!
Then read it some more!

Warrior Bride, Warrior Bride!
It's time to search
Both far and near,
For people ready,
To fight not fear!

Warrior Bride, Warrior Bride!
It's time to write the vision!
Make it plain Warrior Bride!
This is your mission!

Warrior Bride, Warrior Bride!
It's time to work!
Don't stop now!
Press hard Warrior Bride,
It won't hurt!

Warrior Bride, Warrior Bride!
There's no time to waste!
The time is far spent!
It's getting late!

Warrior Bride, Warrior Bride!
It's time to move ahead!
You already know,
Faith without works is dead!

Warrior Bride, Warrior Bride!
It's no time to quit!
Reach up for God's hand,
You can, make it!

Warrior Bride, Warrior Bride!
It's time to hear!
Your first love is calling you!
Come closer, come near!

Warrior Bride, Warrior Bride!
It's time to rise and shine!
Come forth my Church Bride,
No time to hide!
I am your first Love,
And you, you are Mine!

8/19/2018

WHAT IS CHRISTMAS?

*It's not a Holy Day,
Like the Passover Seder.
We partake of His body,
To remember, our Savior.*

*It's not a Holy Day,
Like the Feast of Unleavened Bread.
A time when Christ died on the cross,
In our stead.*

*It's not a Holy Day,
Like the Feast of Trumpets.
A signal for His return,
He will, come back for us.*

*It's not a Holy Day,
Like some, claim it to be,
No Atonement on that day, will we see.*

*It's not a Holy Day,
Like the Feast of Tabernacles.
A festival of booths and tents,
Just for GOD's people.*

*CHRISTMAS DAY for some,
is just another party day.
But the truth will be told,
on God's Last Great, Holy Day.*

*ON CHRISTMAS DAY...
There is no heart felt worship, on their knees,
Just trimming and decking,
Their Christmas trees.*

*A day of multi-colored lights,
Blinking and twinkling,
all through the night.
But when you know Jesus,
You know, that's not right!*

*ON CHRISTMAS DAY ...
People wake and they fake.
But when you know Jesus, you know,
That is not, the path to take!*

*What would Jesus say,
About Christmas Day?
He would say,
It's not the way, or the truth, or the life,
we should display!*

So get to know Jesus, before it's too late,
And you'll find out, that no one knows,
His true, BIRTH - DATE.

That is without a doubt,
what we really should say,
Because CHRISTMAS really is,
a man-made, pagan, holiday.

12/28/11

> I hate, I despise
> your feast days,
> and I will not smell in your
> solemn assemblies.
> Amos 5:21

WHO IS MY SOULMATE?

*I hear Him.
I feel Him.
I know that He's near.*

*But who is my Soulmate?
He knew me before I was born.
I hear Him.
I feel Him.
I know that He's near.*

*Who is my Soulmate?
He says that I'm beautifully
and wonderfully made.
I hear Him.
I feel Him.
I know that He's near.*

*Who is my Soulmate?
He says that I am a royal priesthood.
I hear Him.
I feel Him.
I know that He's near.*

Who is my Soulmate?
When He says I'm more than a conqueror,
I honor His Word.
I hear Him.
I feel Him.
I know that He's near.

But Who is my Soulmate?
He tells me that I am the head
and not the tail.
But, I look to Him as my head,
Because I hear Him.
And I feel Him.
And I know that He's near.

Who is my Soulmate?
His Word says that I am above
and not beneath.

But I am so glad that He is high above,
and looking down on me.
I hear Him.
I feel Him.
I know that He's near.

Who is my Soulmate?
He covers me with His blood
and fills me with his love.
So I can hear Him.
I can feel Him.
I know that He's near.

But who is my Soulmate?
The lover of your soul says He!

I hear Him!
He's the one that died on the cross,
Just for me!

As I draw nigh to Him,
I feel Him, draw nigh to me!
There is nothing to fear,
Because I know that He's near.

My Redeemer is my Soulmate!

I Praise Him!
Because He has always been,
Right here!

7-30-2012

A SPIRITURAL MOTHER

*A spiritual mother
is a special kind of mother!
She doesn't have natural power,
to fly up in the sky.
But she can tear down
strongholds in the spirit,
With her supernatural power,
from on high!*

*No, she can't leap tall buildings,
in a single bound!
But she can send the Word
to heal someone, in a far away town.*

*She doesn't have a cookbook,
Nope, there is no need for one!
Because she feeds her children from
"GOD'S GOOD BOOK"!
Yep, that's the one!*

*A spiritual mother is
wise and smart.
Because she has a mothers,
Kind and loving heart.*

But nothing can beat her powerful prayers!
They hold back the rain.
They even, stop pain.
Praise God! We're healed again!

We love our spiritual mother.
Not because of her supernatural power,
But because she loved us first, just like God,
Our spiritual Father.

Do you have a spiritual mother?
I advise you to get one today!
She can help you to grow up,
the right, spiritual way!
Then you can be a blessing,
to your spiritual mother,
on her birthday!

7/15/2007

> Children, obey your parents in all things: for this is well pleasing unto the Lord.
> Colossians 3:20

EL ELYON

Who is higher, then El Elyon?
No one, no one!
Who is greater then El Elyon?
No one, no one!

El Elyon is the
Most High Elohim,
Forever and forever!

No one is higher then El Elyon
No one, no one!
No one is greater
Then El Elyon!
No one, no one!

El Elyon can never fail!
Who else can make that claim?
No one, no one!
Because no one is higher then El Elyon!
No one, no one!
No one is greater
Then El Elyon!
No one, no one!
Who can hold the sun in place?
Who can raise the Son of grace?

No one, no one!
No one is mightier
Then El Elyon,
No one, no one!
No one is worthy like El Elyon,
No one, no one!

Who deserves praise
More than El Elyon?
No one, no one!
Who deserves glory
More than El Elyon?
No one, not one!
Who deserves honor
More than El Elyon?
No one, absolutely no one!

El Elyon is the
Most high Elohim!
El Elyon will always be,
The Most High King!

Give praise! Give glory!
And Give Honor!
To the one and only
King of Kings!

He is full of mercy,
And full of grace!
No one, absolutely no one,
Can ever, take His place!
Who is higher then
Our El Elyon?
No one, no one!

6/21/18

> Great and marvellous are thy works, Lord God Almighty.
>
> Revelation 15:3

I BLESS YOU, MY ELOHIM

My Elohim, My Elohim,
Ani Barach Ata, My Elohim!
My Elohim, My Elohim,
Ani, Barach Ata!
For your ahava, I live My Elohim.
Ani Barach Ata My Elohim!
For your unconditional ahava,
I live!

My Elohim, My Elohim,
Ani Barach Ata, My Elohim!
My Elohim, My Elohim,
Ani, Barach Ata!
For your mercy, I live My Elohim.
Ani Barach Ata My Elohim!
Because I enjoy your tender mercies,
everyday.

My Elohim, My Elohim,
Ani Barach Ata, My Elohim!
My Elohim, My Elohim, Ani, Barach Ata!
For your compassion, I live My Elohim.
Ani Barach Ata My Elohim!
Your compassion is felt deep within my lev.

My Elohim, My Elohim,
Ani Barach Ata, My Elohim!
My Elohim, My Elohim, Ani, Barach Ata!
Because of your grace, I live My Elohim.
Ani Barach Ata! Ani Barak Ata!
Ani Barach Ata My Elohim,
Because Your grace refreshes my soul!

My Elohim, My Elohim,
Ani Barach Ata, My Elohim!
My Elohim, My Elohim, Ani, Barach Ata!
For your favor, I live My Elohim.
Ani Barach Ata, My Elohim!
Even when I waver,
your favor remains for me!

My Elohim, My Elohim,
Ani Barach Ata, My Elohim!
My Elohim, My Elohim, Ani, Barach Ata!
Only in your presence My Elohim,
Your ahava surrounds me.
Only in your presence My Elohim,
Your mercy abounds me.
Only in your presence My Elohim,
Your compassion fills me.
Only in your presence My Elohim,
Your grace is sufficient for me.
Only in your presence My Elohim,
Your favor awaits me.

Ani Barach Ata, My Elohim!
Ani Barach Ata!

My Elohim, My Elohim,
Ani Barach Ata, My Elohim!
My Elohim, My Elohim,
Ani Barach Ata!
Ani Barach Ata
Always and forever,
My Elohim!
Because "You" Are My Elohim,
Ani Barach Ata!

2/1/ 2018

> Bless the LORD,
> O my soul:
> and all that is within me,
> bless his holy name.
> Psalm 103:1

STRENGTHEN ME O ELOHIM

Strengthen me O Elohim
For the task ahead,
I need your help, I must be lead!

Strengthen me O Elohim
I can't do this alone,
I need your help, please guide me, Shalom!

Strengthen me O Elohim
To make this decision.
I really need your help,
To complete this mission.

Strengthen me O Elohim
From my head to my toe!
I need your help, I'm sure, you know.

Strengthen me O Elohim
To walk in your will.
I need your help, to even be still

Strengthen me O Elohim
From day til night.
I really need your help,
to pray and not fright.

*Strengthen me O Elohim
In my inner man.
I need help, to follow your plan!*

*Strengthen me O Elohim
I look only to you!
I need your help My Elohim,
and Lord Yeshua's too!
Amen!*

12/20/2012

> O Lord GOD,
> remember me, I pray thee,
> and strengthen me,
> I pray thee
> Judges 16:28

Dr. Kathleen B. Oden

Dr. Kathleen B. Oden is an author, missionary and Bible teacher, at God's House of Refuge Church & School of Evangelism. She attained a Doctorate degree in Christian Theology in 2000.

After a bad fall in 2014, she realized that she had to start eating healthy, in order to fully recover. She became a Certified Health Minister and God gave her a ministry called, Create Anewu Health Ministry.

Dr. Oden loves ministering to people and her health ministry has opened the door for her to share what the WORD OF GOD has to say, about eating healthy food.

She has published over 20 books through Amazon.com. Some are Christian, several on Hebrew training and several about health, wellness and essential oils.

Dr. Oden is currently working on a book called The Old Testament Synopsis, which will be published in 2019.

****
****
******

LITERARY WORKS

1998 THE HOLY SPIRIT *(Masters Degree Thesis)*
2000 About The Bible *(Doctorate Degree Thesis)*
2004 The Old Testament *(Synopsis)*
2005 What God Commanded - *pub.:2015*
2006 The New Testament *(Synopsis)*

2012 Hebrew Training Manual & Workbook - *published:2015*
2012 Aleph-Bet Story & Workbook *published:2015*
2012 Biblical Hebrew & Aleph-Bet Workbook - *published:2015*

2015 All About The Bible *published:2015*
2015 21 Day Weight Loss Challenge *(3 book series) - published:2015*
2015 Create A New You In Only 90-Days *published:2015*
2015 How To Lose Weight Fast Without Exercising - *published:2015*
2015 One True Love - *published: 2017*

2016 O.T. Bible Stories (Gen. - Deu.) - *published:2016*
2016 O.T. Bible Stories (Jos. - Chr.) - *published:2016*
2016 Learning The Books of The Bible In 10 Easy Lessons - *published:2016*

2016 Healthy Eating, Weight Loss & Wellness - published:2016
2016 3 Day Energizing & Cleansing Detox
published:2016
2016 How To Use Essential Oils
published:2016
2016 Create Anewu Healthy Creations
published:2016

EMAIL:
createanewu@consultant.com

WEBSITE:
teachingbythespirit@minister.com

WEBSITE:
www.createanewuhealthministry.com

Made in the USA
Columbia, SC
12 October 2020